ENGINEERING MARVELS

FIGHTER JETS

Marne Ventura

LIGHTB◆X
openlightbox.com

LIGHTBOX

Go to
www.openlightbox.com
and enter this book's
unique code.

ACCESS CODE

L B N 2 7 7 3 7

Lightbox is an all-inclusive digital solution for the teaching and learning of curriculum topics in an original, groundbreaking way. Lightbox is based on National Curriculum Standards.

STANDARD FEATURES OF LIGHTBOX

 AUDIO High-quality narration using text-to-speech system

 VIDEOS Embedded high-definition video clips

 ACTIVITIES Printable PDFs that can be emailed and graded

 WEBLINKS Curated links to external, child-safe resources

SLIDESHOWS Pictorial overviews of key concepts

 TRANSPARENCIES Step-by-step layering of maps, diagrams, charts, and timelines

 INTERACTIVE MAPS Interactive maps and aerial satellite imagery

 QUIZZES Ten multiple choice questions that are automatically graded and emailed for teacher assessment

 KEY WORDS Matching key concepts to their definitions

Contents

Chapter 1

Streaking Across the Sky

Ethan moved to the front of the bleachers and looked to his right. First he heard a rumble. Then he saw it. Nine fighter jets were flying in formation. They streaked over the crowd at the air show. Ethan cheered. The jets' power and speed was unlike anything he had seen before.

More than 10,000 jets and airplanes fly at Wisconsin's annual EAA AirVenture Oshkosh, one of the largest air shows in the world.

Fighter jets are used by militaries. They are small, fast, jet-powered planes. A typical jet carries one or two people. Fighter jets also carry weapons, such as bombs or missiles. Different jets have different purposes. Some fight other aircraft in the air. Some are designed to attack targets on the ground. Some accompany other aircraft carrying supplies or people. Fighter jets defend these aircraft in case of attack.

Armies used propeller airplanes during World War I (1914–1918). Pilots often used handguns to fight enemies. Airplanes became more advanced during World War II (1939–1945). In 1944, the German military fought with Me 262s. They were the first fighter planes with jet engines. Fighter jets were much faster than propeller airplanes.

The U.S. Air Force had to catch up. Engineers at Lockheed Corporation in California made the P-80 Shooting Star.

The P-80 Shooting Star can fly about 1,000 miles (1,600 kilometers) before having to land.

Sun Air Parts

PlanesOfFame.org

PACEMAKER

100

The **Lockheed Corporation** is more than **100 years old**.

The **Me 262's** top speed is **559 miles per hour** (900 km/h).

During **World War II**, the **United States** made more than **300,000** airplanes.

F-16 Fighting Falcons have a combat range of about 500 miles (800 km). Refueling in the air extends their range, helping them go on longer missions.

Lockheed designed and built the plane in only 143 days. The P-80 Shooting Star was still being tested in August 1945, about a month before World War II ended. But the Shooting Star was used in the Korean War (1950–1953).

In total, 1,715 Shooting Stars were built. They flew approximately 500 miles per hour (805 km/h) and carried six machine guns. They also carried either 10 rockets or a large bomb.

Fighter jets continue to get better with new technology. Today's fighter jets are fast and strong. But they are also lightweight and **maneuverable**. Some even have the ability to refuel in the air. New technology helps pilots **navigate** and communicate. It also helps them find or avoid enemies during the night or day, in any weather. New designs and materials also make **stealth** jets possible.

Chapter 2

Fighter Jet Design

Most fighter jets have the same basic design. Wings lift the plane off the ground, allowing it to fly. Vertical and horizontal stabilizers form the tail of the plane. Stabilizers help control the plane's direction of flight. Movable parts on the wings and tail control the plane's altitude. Jet engines move the plane forward.

France's Dassault Rafale fighter jet has a top speed of 1,190 miles per hour (1,915 km/h) and a maximum range of 1,150 miles (1,850 km).

Additional parts support the plane while on the ground, taking off, or landing. The body, or fuselage, holds the pilot. The cockpit is where the pilot sits. This area contains the controls for the jet. Meanwhile, weapons are located in different parts of the plane, such as hanging from the wings or fuselage.

An aircraft is heavier than air. This means the force of **gravity** keeps it on the ground. So, planes must overcome the force of gravity through thrust and lift.

Gravity is **weaker** high in the air. Twelve miles (19 km) up, an F-22 jet would weigh about **320 pounds** (145 kilograms) less.

The **fastest** jet, the **SR-71 Blackbird,** reaches **2,193 miles** per hour (3,529 km/h).

Some jet speeds are measured by **Mach** number. **Mach 1** is the speed of sound, about **760 miles** per hour (1,223 km/h). Mach 2 is twice that.

Jet engines create thrust. Air is sucked into the front of the engine with a large fan. Once inside, the air is **compressed** and mixed with jet fuel. Sparks ignite the fuel. This causes burning gas to shoot out the back of the engine. Thrust pushes the jet forward so lift from the wings can overcome the weight of the jet. Thrust also overcomes **drag** created by **friction** with the air.

Jets with twin engines are called "heavy fighters." The extra engine gives them enough power to carry heavier weapons.

The F-15E Strike Eagle has a maximum takeoff weight of 81,000 pounds (36,741 kg).

Jets are made of strong but light materials. This means there is less weight to overcome. Aluminum, steel, titanium, and fiberglass are all common materials.

Wings create lift. Their shape makes air flow faster over the top of the wing than it flows under the bottom. The air pressure on top of the wing is less than the air pressure under the wing. This pressure difference pushes the jet up.

Pilots need to make sharp turns at high speeds without losing control. Flaps, rudders, and other movable parts on the wings and tail change the way air moves around the aircraft. Pilots move these parts to make the plane change direction. Modern jets have computer systems that display information on the cockpit windshield. This allows pilots to keep their heads up at all times rather than having to look down at a control panel.

Fighter jets use radar to locate targets. Radar works by using radio waves. The waves bounce off of objects. Stealth jets are able to avoid being detected by radar. They are designed with angled surfaces and covered with a special paint. These features prevent radio waves from bouncing back toward the radar source.

The B-2 bomber is known for its stealth design and construction.

Engineering Design Process

Engineers make sure the fighter jets they design are safe and effective. When they are satisfied with their design, the fighter jet is built.

ASK What features are needed for a fighter jet? Which shape works best? Which materials are strongest and lightest?

IMAGINE Brainstorm ideas for fighter jet designs. Make a list of important features.

PLAN Draw a diagram of a fighter jet. Make a list of materials needed. Write down the steps to build the jet.

CREATE Follow the plan and build the fighter jet. Make a test flight. Does it perform as expected?

IMPROVE How could the design change to make it better? Try it again!

Chapter 3

The Harrier jet can go from 620 miles per hour (1,000 km/h) to a complete stop in 12 seconds.

Building a Fighter Jet

Most fighter jets take off and land by rolling down a long, flat runway. But runways aren't always available. So in the 1960s, British engineers designed and built the Harrier fighter jet.

The jet can take off by flying straight up. It lands by coming straight down. This allows it to operate from small spaces.

The Harrier can take off and land from dirt roads or on short runways, such as a ship. The plane can also hover like a helicopter. It can fly sideways, backward, and even turn in place in midair.

To make these jets work, engineers added engine exhaust nozzles to different places on the fuselage. These nozzles can swivel to change the direction of the thrust from the engine. To move the jet straight up, the exhaust nozzles point downward. Gas shoots out toward the ground, which pushes the jet up. Changing the direction of different nozzles lets the pilot move in different directions.

Engineers also used a special shape for Harrier fighter jets. The extra-broad wings are on top of the fuselage. They angle downward and have round edges. This shape helps the plane fly straight up or down. Movable flaps on the tail and wings also help steer a Harrier jet.

The AV-8B Harrier II Plus has swept wings, which angle backward. With less drag, the plane can fly faster.

Chapter 4

The F/A-18 Super Hornet is flown by pilots of the U.S. Navy and the Royal Australian Air Force.

The Super Hornet

The Super Hornet F/A-18 is the first U.S. plane designed with the ability to be both a fighter (F) and attack (A) jet. It is built for air-to-air combat with other jets. It is also built to fire weapons from the air toward targets on the ground or at sea.

The F/A-18 has a strong airframe and landing gear. This allows it to take off and land on an **aircraft carrier**. Its wings are trapezoid shaped and swept back. This gives the plane better performance. In addition, the Super Hornet has a heads-up display and a high-thrust engine. Meanwhile, the Super Hornet has attack features, including missiles and a cannon. The jet can also fly at **supersonic** speed in any weather.

Mapping Fighter Jets

The United States is home to one of the strongest air forces in the world, with thousands of fighter jets. The map shows where some of these engineering marvels are found, and where pilots are trained to fly them. Can you see any fighter jets near where you live?

Military Aviation Museum
Virginia Beach, Virginia

One of the largest collections of military aircraft can be found at the Military Aviation Museum in Virginia. Visitors can see planes from both World Wars, watch air shows, and even fly in a historical fighter jet.

Edwards Air Force Base
Southern California

Edwards Air Force Base outside of Los Angeles, California, is home to the largest air runway in the country. The 15,000-foot (4,600-meter) runway is used by fighter jets—and was once even used by space shuttles.

2

Naval Air Station Pensacola
Pensacola, Florida

The U.S. Navy's flight demonstration squad, the Blue Angels, was founded in 1946. Since then, more than 260 million people have watched them fly F/A-18 Hornets during air shows across the country.

1

UNITED STATES

Atlantic Ocean

3

Pacific Ocean

Hawai'i
100 Miles
0   161 Kilometers

Legend
- Water
- Land
- United States

N
W   E
S

250 Miles
0   402 Kilometers

Alaska

500 Miles
0   804 Kilometers

Timeline

Today, fighter jets streak across the skies of the United States. These pieces of advanced technology are used by pilots to serve and protect the country every day. Discover more about the history of U.S. fighter jets and their pilots.

1914–1918

Flying British and French planes, American pilots, including "Arizona Balloon Buster" Frank Luke and "Ace of Aces" Eddie Rickenbacker, become famous for their air fighting skills during World War I.

1916

William E. Boeing founds Aero Products Company in Seattle, Washington. It later becomes the Boeing Company, one of the largest producers of fighter jets in the world.

1947

The U.S. Air Force is created within the Department of Defense. It is responsible for air warfare, defense, and research.

1960s

Boeing's F-4 Phantom II becomes the primary American fighter jet. It is used by the U.S. Air Force, U.S. Navy, and U.S. Marine Corps.

1991

Advanced fighter jet technology, such as laser-guided missiles and GPS, helps the United States and its allies win the Persian Gulf War.

2017

The Lockheed Martin Corporation begins work to upgrade the F-22 Raptor and F-35 Lightning II, which are considered to be the most advanced fighter jets in the world. Improvements are being made to stealth capabilities, firepower, and computer software.

Fighter Jet Challenge

Now it is your turn to build an airplane. Use the information you've learned about **aerodynamics** to design and build a paper glider.

Materials

For this challenge, you'll need scissors and paper clips. You'll also need paper of different thicknesses or weights.

Procedure

Use these directions to build two paper airplanes. Start one by folding the paper the long way. Start the other by folding the paper the short way.

1. Fold the paper in half. Open the paper to lie flat again.

2. On one end, fold both corners in to the center crease. This creates a point.

3. Make the point even sharper by folding both angled edges in to the center crease again.

4. Close the paper along the centerline crease. Fold each side down to create wings. The edge of the part you are folding down should be parallel with the bottom of the fuselage.

5. Fold the wings partly back up so they are horizontal, with the fuselage vertical beneath them.

6. Launch the airplane!

Improve It!

Which shape flew faster and farther?

Are there different ways you could fold the nose and wings to make these parts better?

- Try cutting flaps or notches at different places in the wings, especially along the trailing edges.

- Adjust the weight and balance of the glider. Try adding paper clips to different places. Which locations result in the best overall performance of the glider?

- Try using lighter or heavier paper.

Quiz

1 How many people does a fighter jet carry?

2 What were the first fighter planes with jet engines?

3 In which war was the P-80 Shooting Star used?

4 Which parts of the plane help control its flight direction?

5 What are fighter jets with twin engines called?

6 How fast is Mach 1?

7 Is the air pressure on top of the wing more or less than the air pressure under the wing?

8 What do fighter jets use to locate targets?

9 Which jet can take off by flying straight up?

10 Where is the longest air runway in the United States located?

Answers

1. One or two **2.** Me 262s **3.** Korean War **4.** Stabilizers **5.** Heavy fighters **6.** The speed of sound, about 760 miles per hour (1,223 km/h) **7.** Less **8.** Radar **9.** Harrier jet **10.** Edwards Air Force Base

Key Words

aerodynamics: the qualities of an object that affect how easily it is able to move through the air

aircraft carrier: a warship on which aircraft can take off and land

compressed: pressed or squeezed together

drag: a force that resists motion through a gas, like air, or through a fluid, like water

friction: the resistance of one surface against another

gravity: the force due to the mass of the Earth that pulls objects downward

maneuverable: able to change direction easily and quickly

navigate: to find one's way while traveling

stealth: designed to avoid being noticed

supersonic: moving faster than the speed of sound

Index

LIGHTB◆X

⊕ SUPPLEMENTARY RESOURCES

Click on the plus icon ⊕ found in the bottom left corner of each spread to open additional teacher resources.

- Download and print the book's quizzes and activities
- Access curriculum correlations
- Explore additional web applications that enhance the Lightbox experience

LIGHTBOX DIGITAL TITLES
Packed full of integrated media

VIDEOS

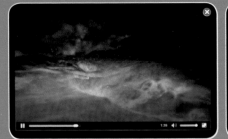

INTERACTIVE MAPS

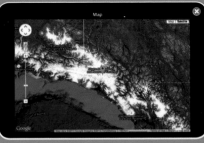

WEBLINKS

SLIDESHOWS

QUIZZES

OPTIMIZED FOR
✓ **TABLETS**
✓ **WHITEBOARDS**
✓ **COMPUTERS**
✓ **AND MUCH MORE!**

Published by Smartbook Media Inc.
350 5th Avenue, 59th Floor New York, NY 10118
Website: www.openlightbox.com

Library of Congress Control Number: 2017961991

ISBN 978-1-5105-3730-9 (hardcover)
ISBN 978-1-5105-3731-6 (multi-user eBook)

Printed in the Brainerd, Minnesota, United States
1 2 3 4 5 6 7 8 9 0 22 21 20 19 18

First published by North Star Editions in 2018.

Project Coordinator: Jared Siemens
Designer: Ana María Vidal

Every reasonable effort has been made to trace ownership and to obtain permission to reprint copyright material. The publisher would be pleased to have any errors or omissions brought to its attention so that they may be corrected in subsequent printings.

The publisher acknowledges Alamy, Newscom, Getty Images, iStock, and Shutterstock as the primary image suppliers for this title.